TRANZLATY

Lingua est pro omnibus

Language is for everyone

Parva Syreni

The Little Mermaid

Hans Christian Andersen

Latin / English

Copyright © 2023 Tranzlaty
All rights reserved.
Published by Tranzlaty
ISBN: 978-1-83566-954-9
Original text by Hans Christian Andersen
Den Lille Havfrue
First published in Danish in 1837
www.tranzlaty.com

Palatium Regis Maris
The Sea King's Palace

Absit in oceano, ubi aqua caerulea est
Far out in the ocean, where the water is blue
hic aqua tam caerulea quam pulcherrima cornflower
here the water is as blue as the prettiest cornflower
et aqua tam clarissima quam purissima cristallus
and the water is as clear as the purest crystal
haec aqua, procul in Oceano est valde profunda
this water, far out in the ocean is very, very deep
aqua adeo profunda est, ut nulla funis ad fundum pervenire possit
water so deep, indeed, that no cable could reach the bottom
Ecclesia multa loca super se struere posset
you could pile many church steeples upon each other
Sed non omnes ecclesiae superficies aquarum
but all the churches could not reach the surface of the water
Ibi habitant mare regem et subditos suos
There dwell the Sea King and his subjects
putes iustum harenam luteam fundo
you might think it is just bare yellow sand at the bottom
sed nihil esse ibi putandum est
but we must not imagine that there is nothing there
in hac arena mirabiles flores et plantae crescunt
on this sand grow the strangest flowers and plants
et non potes imaginari quam lenta folia et caules sint
and you can't imagine how pliant the leaves and stems are
levis agitatio aquae facit folia movere
the slightest agitation of the water causes the leaves to stir
est sicut unumquodque folium habet vitam suam
it is as if each leaf had a life of its own
Pisces maiores et minores inter ramos labentur
Fishes, both large and small, glide between the branches
sicut cum aves inter arbores hic ad terram volant
just like when birds fly among the trees here upon land

In altissimo omnium loco stat pulcrum castrum
In the deepest spot of all stands a beautiful castle
hoc pulcherrimum castrum est arx Regis maris
this beautiful castle is the castle of the Sea King
moenibus castelli edificantur curalium
the walls of the castle are built of coral
et fenestrae gothicae longae sunt ex electri lucidissimo
and the long Gothic windows are of the clearest amber
Tectum castri ex conchis marinis
The roof of the castle is formed of sea shells
et conchilia aperta et proxima sicut aqua super eos defluit
and the shells open and close as the water flows over them
Eorum species pulchrior est quam describi potest
Their appearance is more beautiful than can be described
in unaquaque testa jacet micans margarita
within each shell there lies a glittering pearl
et quaevis margarita sit aptum diadema reginae
and each pearl would be fit for the diadem of a queen

Rex mare multos annos viduus fuerat
The Sea King had been a widower for many years
materque anus curaque domestica
and his aged mother looked after the household for him
Illa erat valde sensibilis mulier
She was a very sensible woman
sed erat superbissima de genere regio
but she was exceedingly proud of her royal birth
et propterea utebatur in cauda sua duodecim ostrea
and on that account she wore twelve oysters on her tail
alii nobiles tantum sex ostrea induere permiserunt
others of high rank were only allowed to wear six oysters
Erat autem dignissimos maxime laudantium
She was, however, deserving of very great praise
est quod illa maxime laudari
there was something she especially deserved praise for

et suscepit parvam maris reginae magna cura
she took great care of the little sea princesses
et habebat sex neptes eam amavit
she had six granddaughters that she loved
mare reginae pulchrae liberos
all the sea princesses were beautiful children
princeps autem minimus maris erat pulcherrimus eorum
but the youngest sea princess was the prettiest of them
Pellis eius tam clara erat et gracilis sicut folium rosae
Her skin was as clear and delicate as a rose leaf
et oculi eius tam caerulei quam profundissimum mare
and her eyes were as blue as the deepest sea
sed, ut cetera, pedes non habebat
but, like all the others, she had no feet
et in fine corporis eius cauda piscis erat
and at the end of her body was a fish's tail

Tota die in magnis castri luserunt atria
All day long they played in the great halls of the castle
e moenibus castelli florum pulchri
out of the walls of the castle grew beautiful flowers
et amavit ludere inter vivos flores
and she loved to play among the living flowers
Fenestrae electri magnae apertae sunt et pisces natabant
The large amber windows were open, and the fish swam in
id est sicut cum fenestras apertas relinquimus
it is just like when we leave the windows open
tum pulchrae hirundines in nostras aedes volant
and then the pretty swallows fly into our houses
tantum pisces ad reginae natant
only the fishes swam up to the princesses
soli comederunt e manibus eius
they were the only ones that ate out of her hands
et permiserunt se ab illa permulcere
and they allowed themselves to be stroked by her

Extra castrum hortus erat pulcherrimus
Outside the castle there was a beautiful garden
in horto creverunt flores rubei et atro-caerulei
in the garden grew bright-red and dark-blue flowers
et effloruit sicut flamma ignis
and there grew blossoms like flames of fire
fructus in plantis fulgentes sicut aurum
the fruit on the plants glittered like gold
et folia et caules continue agitaverunt huc atque illuc
and the leaves and stems continually waved to and fro
terra in terra erat arenae optimae
The earth on the ground was the finest sand
sed haec arena non habet colorem arenae novimus
but this sand does not have the colour of the sand we know
Haec arena tam caerulea est quam flamma ardentis sulphuris
this sand is as blue as the flame of burning sulphur
Singula caerulea super omnia ponere jubar
Over everything lay a peculiar blue radiance
est sicut caelum caeruleum ubique
it is as if the blue sky were everywhere
de hyacintho de caelo et supra et infra
the blue of the sky was above and below
In tranquillo tempestate sol videri poterat
In calm weather the sun could be seen
hinc sol instar floris rubro-purpurei
from here the sun looked like a reddish-purple flower
et lux e calyce floris fluxit
and the light streamed from the calyx of the flower

hortus palatii in plures partes divisus est
the palace garden was divided into several parts
Uterque autem principes habebat proprium agellum
Each of the princesses had their own little plot of ground
hoc pacto possent serere quidquid florum vellent
on this plot they could plant whatever flowers they pleased
unus princeps disposita flore suo in forma cete

one princess arranged her flower bed in the form of a whale
unus princeps flores quasi parum syreni
one princess arranged her flowers like a little mermaid
et fecit minimus puer hortum suum rotundum sicut sol
and the youngest child made her garden round, like the sun
et in horto suo flores rubicundos creverunt
and in her garden grew beautiful red flowers
Hi flores rubri erant sicut radii solis
these flowers were as red as the rays of the sunset

Erat enim puer alienus; quietam et cogitationem
She was a strange child; quiet and thoughtful
sororibus eius mirabilia delectabantur
her sisters showed delight at the wonderful things
quae ex naufragiis vasorum
the things they obtained from the wrecks of vessels
sed curabat tantum sibi satis rubicundis floribus
but she cared only for her pretty red flowers
quamquam erat etiam statua marmorea pulchra
although there was also a beautiful marble statue
simulacrum erat repraesentatio formosi pueri
the statue was the representation of a handsome boy
puer sculptus erat ex lapide albo puro
the boy had been carved out of pure white stone
et simulacrum ad imum mare de naufragio cecidisset
and the statue had fallen to the bottom of the sea from a wreck
ad hoc pueri marmoreum simulacrum de eo curabat
for this marble statue of a boy she cared about too

Plantavit per simulacrum , Rosarium flentem salicis
She planted, by the statue, a rose-colored weeping willow
mox et flens super statuae ramos recentia salix pependit
and soon the weeping willow hung its fresh branches over the statue
rami paene usque ad caeruleam arenam
the branches almost reached down to the blue sands

umbrae arboris colorem violaceum
The shadows of the tree had the color of violet
et umbrae huc atque illuc sicut rami
and the shadows waved to and fro like the branches
Haec omnia creavit maxime interesting illusio
all of this created the most interesting illusion
est sicut corona arboris et radices ludit
it was as if the crown of the tree and the roots were playing
Videbatur si quaerunt osculari se
it looked as if they were trying to kiss each other

ea summa voluptas audiebat de mundo supra
her greatest pleasure was hearing about the world above
mundi super altum mare quae habitabat
the world above the deep sea she lived in
Aviam suam fecit ei de omnibus supernis nuntiare
She made her old grandmother tell her all about the upper world
naves et oppida, homines et animalia
the ships and the towns, the people and the animals
illic flores terræ fragrantia
up there the flowers of the land had fragrance
flores infra mare non habebant odorem
the flowers below the sea had no fragrance
ibi arbores silvae virides
up there the trees of the forest were green
et pisces in arboribus pulchre cantare potuerunt
and the fishes in the trees could sing beautifully
ibi voluptatem audire piscem
up there it was a pleasure to listen to the fish
aviam piscibus avibus appellaverunt
her grandmother called the birds fishes
alioquin pusillus syreni non intellexisset
else the little mermaid would not have understood
quia numquam visae aves parvae syreni
because the little mermaid had never seen birds

aviam ei de ritibus Nereidum
her grandmother told her about the rites of mermaids
"Unus die pervenies ad annum quintum decimum"
"one day you will reach your fifteenth year"
"Tunc licebit ire ad superficiem"
"then you will have permission to go to the surface"
"Potestis sedere super scopulos in luce lunae"
"you will be able to sit on the rocks in the moonlight"
" et naves magnas navigantes videbis "
"and you will see the great ships go sailing by"
"Tunc videbis silvas et oppida et populos";
"Then you will see forests and towns and the people"

Sequenti anno una sororum quindecim futurarum erat
the following year one of the sisters was going to be fifteen
sed unaquaque soror fuit anno iunior quam alter
but each sister was a year younger than the other
minimus soror iret ad quinquennium expectaturus antequam eam vice
the youngest sister was going to have to wait five years before her turn
nisi tunc posset surgere ab imo ad Oceanum
only then could she rise up from the bottom of the ocean
et tunc solum poterat videre terram sicut nos
and only then could she see the earth as we do
Sed unaquaeque sororum sibi invicem promittit
However, each of the sisters made each other a promise
nunciaturi erant aliis quod viderant
they were going to tell the others what they had seen
Avia eorum non satis indicare
Their grandmother could not tell them enough
tot res scire volebant
there were so many things they wanted to know about

minimus soror ad eam convertat maxime concupivit

the youngest sister longed for her turn the most
sed diutius quam ceteri omnes exspectare debebant
but, she had to wait longer than all the others
et haec tam quieta et cogitata de mundo
and she was so quiet and thoughtful about the world
multae noctes erant ubi adfuit fenestra aperta
there were many nights where she stood by the open window
et suspexit per caerula caerula
and she looked up through the dark blue water
et piscem spectabat ut pinnulis suis spargebant
and she watched the fish as they splashed with their fins
Videret lunam et stellas languide lucentes
She could see the moon and stars shining faintly
sed de profundo sub aqua haec aliter spectant
but from deep below the water these things look different
lunam et stellas maiores quam ad oculos
the moon and stars looked larger than they do to our eyes
interdum quasi nubes nigra abiit praeteritum
sometimes, something like a black cloud went past
sciebat se posse esse balaenam natantem super caput eius
she knew that it could be a whale swimming over her head
vel posset esse navis plena hominum
or it could be a ship, full of human beings
homines qui non poterant imaginari quid sub illis
human beings who couldn't imagine what was under them
satis parum syreni manus alba tenens manum eius
a pretty little mermaid holding out her white hands
satis parva syreni tendens ad navem
a pretty little mermaid reaching towards their ship

Sororum in Parva syreni
The Little Mermaid's Sisters

Dies venit, ubi maior Syrena eius natalem decimum quintum habuit
The day came when the eldest mermaid had her fifteenth birthday
nunc permissum est ad superficiem Oceani
now she was allowed to rise to the surface of the ocean
et illa nocte natavit usque ad superficiem
and that night she swum up to the surface
potes imaginari omnia quae vidit illic
you can imagine all the things she saw up there
et potes cogitare omnia quae habuit loqui
and you can imagine all the things she had to talk about
Sed optimum , inquit , in arena iacebat
But the finest thing, she said, was to lie on a sand bank
in quietam lunam maris, prope litus
in the quiet moonlit sea, near the shore
inde lumina in terram
from there she had gazed at the lights on the land
lumina erant prope oppidum
they were the lights of the near-by town
lumina quasi stellae centum twinkled
the lights had twinkled like hundreds of stars
quae audierat sonos musicorum ab oppido
she had listened to the sounds of music from the town
strepitum curruum equorum ductum audierat
she had heard noise of carriages drawn by their horses
et voces hominum audiverat
and she had heard the voices of human beings
et cum audissent jucunditatem campanarum adulatione
and the had heard merry pealing of the bells
campanas tinnitus in ecclesia deri
the bells ringing in the church steeples
sed haec omnia mirabilia non poterat accedere

but she could not go near all these wonderful things
haec tam mirabilia tanto magis cupiebat
so she longed for these wonderful things all the more

potes imaginari quam cupide sorore minimus audiebat
you can imagine how eagerly the youngest sister listened
descriptiones superorum mundi erant sicut somnium
the descriptions of the upper world were like a dream
postea stetit ad fenestram apertam cubiculi sui
afterwards she stood at the open window of her room
et respexit ad superficiem, per aquam caeruleam
and she looked to the surface, through the dark-blue water
putavit se sororis magnae civitatis esse
she thought of the great city her sister had told her of
civitas magna cum omni strepitu ac strepitu
the great city with all its bustle and noise
si campanarum sonitum audire posset
she even fancied she could hear the sound of the bells
putavit sonum campanarum ad profundum maris deferri
she imagined the sound of the bells carried to the depths of the sea

Post alium annum, secundus soror natalis eius
after another year the second sister had her birthday
ipsa quoque licentia natandi usque ad superficiem
she too received permission to swim up to the surface
et inde natare poterat ubi vellet
and from there she could swim about where she pleased
Ierat ad superficiem sicut sol occumberet
She had gone to the surface just as the sun was setting
hoc, inquit, pulcherrimus omnium aspectus fuit
this, she said, was the most beautiful sight of all
Totum caelum velut orbis ex auro
The whole sky looked like a disk of pure gold
et hyacinthum et nubila rosacea erant
and there were violet and rose-colored clouds

erant pulchra nimis describere, dixit
they were too beautiful to describe, she said
et dixit quomodo nubes ibant per caelum
and she said how the clouds drifted across the sky
et aliquid velocius quam nubila volaverat
and something had flown by more swiftly than the clouds
magna grex olores versus ad occasum
a large flock of wild swans flew toward the setting sun
cygni velut longi coloris trans mare
the swans had been like a long white veil across the sea
Illa etiam ad solem natare conatus erat
She had also tried to swim towards the sun
sol sed longe delapsus in undas
but some distance away the sun sank into the waves
Vidit quomodo roseis colores defluxit de nubibus
she saw how the rosy tints faded from the clouds
et vidit quomodo etiam defluxerat color de mari
and she saw how the colour had also faded from the sea

Sequenti anno tertius sororis tractus erat
the next year it was the third sister's turn
Haec soror omnium sororum audacissima fuit
this sister was the most daring of all the sisters
latum flumen quod evacuavit in mare
she swam up a broad river that emptied into the sea
Ad ripas fluminis vidit colles
On the banks of the river she saw green hills
colles virides pulchris vitibus operti
the green hills were covered with beautiful vines
et in collibus silvae erant arbores
and on the hills there were forests of trees
et extra silvas palatia et castella effossa
and out of the forests palaces and castles poked out
Aves audierat cantantes in arboribus
She had heard birds singing in the trees
radios solis in cute sensit

and she had felt the rays of the sun on her skin
radii tam fortes erant ut retro daretur
the rays were so strong that she had to dive back
et refrixerat ardentem faciem in aqua frigida
and she cooled her burning face in the cool water
In angusto sinus coetus infantum invenit
In a narrow creek she found a group of little children
fuerunt primi hominis filii eam umquam
they were the first human children she had ever seen
Volebat ludere cum filiis quoque
She wanted to play with the children too
filii autem ex ea fugerunt perterriti
but the children fled from her in a great fright
et tunc modicum animal nigrum venit ad aquam
and then a little black animal came to the water
canis erat, sed canem non sciebat
it was a dog, but she did not know it was a dog
quia nunquam viderat canem ante
because she had never seen a dog before
et canem furibundus latrante syreni
and the dog barked at the mermaid furiously
pertimuit et in apertum refugit mare
she became frightened and rushed back to the open sea
Sed dixit se numquam oblivisci silvae pulchrae
But she said she should never forget the beautiful forest
colles virides et bella liberis
the green hills and the pretty children
invenit eam eximie ridiculam quomodo navit
she found it exceptionally funny how they swam
quia non infantes homines parvi caudis
because the little human children didn't have tails
ita cruribus suis calcitrabant aquam
so with their little legs they kicked the water

Quarta soror timidior ultima
The fourth sister was more timid than the last

Illa manere decreverat in medio maris
She had decided to stay in the midst of the sea
sed dixit tam formosa ibi quam propior terra
but she said it was as beautiful there as nearer the land
ex superficie videre poterat multa milia passuum in circuitu eius
from the surface she could see many miles around her
caelum super illam vidi quasi campanulam vitream
the sky above her looked like a bell of glass
et naves navigare viderat
and she had seen the ships sail by
naves autem ab ea longe abesse
but the ships were at a very great distance from her
et, vela secundae, velut mergae marinae
and, with their sails, the ships looked like sea gulls
ut vidit delphinos in undis
she saw how the dolphins played in the waves
et cete grandia effusa aqua e naribus suis
and great whales spouted water from their nostrils
quasi centum fontes omnes ludunt
like a hundred fountains all playing together

Quinta sororis natalis dies in hieme evenit
The fifth sister's birthday occurred in the winter
sic vidit quae ceteri non viderant
so she saw things that the others had not seen
hoc anni tempore mare viride
at this time of the year the sea looked green
magna icebergs natantes viridi aqua
large icebergs were floating on the green water
et unaquaeque iceberg vidi quasi margaritam, dixit
and each iceberg looked like a pearl, she said
sed majores et altiores Ecclesiis
but they were larger and loftier than the churches
erantque maxime interesting formis
and they were of the most interesting shapes

ac quisque iceberg fulgebant sicut crystallini
and each iceberg glittered like diamonds
Sederat se in una ex icebergs
She had seated herself on one of the icebergs
et ventus ludere cum capillis suis
and she let the wind play with her long hair
Animadvertit aliquid interesting de navibus
She noticed something interesting about the ships
omnes naves icebergs celerrime praetervecti sunt
all the ships sailed past the icebergs very rapidly
et eduxerunt quantum possent
and they steered away as far as they could
quasi timerent iceberg
it was as if they were afraid of the iceberg
et mansit in mari usque ad vesperam
she stayed out at sea into the evening
sol occidit et nubes obscura caelum
the sun went down and dark clouds covered the sky
tonitrua advolvit per Oceanum de icebergs
the thunder rolled across the ocean of icebergs
et fulgura fulgura in icebergs
and the flashes of lightning glowed red on the icebergs
et icebergs fluctuante mari
and the icebergs were tossed about by the heaving sea
vela omnium navium trepidabant
the sails of all the ships were trembling with fear
et in fluitante Iceberga sedit syrena placide
and the mermaid sat calmly on the floating iceberg
et aspicit in mare fulmen
and she watched the lightning strike into the sea

Omnes eius quinque sorores maiores iam creverant
All of her five older sisters had grown up now
quare potuerunt ire in superficie cum placuerunt
therefore they could go to the surface when they pleased
primo gaudebant superficie mundi

at first they were delighted with the surface world
non poterant satis novi et pulchrae
they couldn't get enough of the new and beautiful sights
sed omnes denique ad superos indifferentes
but eventually they all grew indifferent towards the upper world
et post mensem multum omnino ultra superficiem mundi non visitaverunt
and after a month they didn't visit the surface world much at all anymore
multo pulchrior erat sorore suae domi
they told their sister it was much more beautiful at home

Saepe tamen horis vespertinis ascenderunt
Yet often, in the evening hours, they did go up
quinque sorores bracchia circum se
the five sisters twined their arms round each other
simulque, bracchio bracchio, surrexerunt
and together, arm in arm, they rose to the surface
sæpe ascenderunt, quando facta est tempestas appropinquans
often they went up when there was a storm approaching
timueruntque ne turbo navem conciliet
they feared that the storm might win a ship
ita adnantes ad navem et ad nautas decantaverunt
so they swam to the vessel and sung to the sailors
Voces eorum erant iucundiores quam ullius hominum
Their voices were more charming than that of any human
et navigantes ne timerent, si decumberent, petierunt
and they begged the voyagers not to fear if they sank
quia profunda maris plena erat deliciarum
because the depths of the sea was full of delights
Sed nautae carmina sua intelligere non potuerunt
But the sailors could not understand their songs
et gemitum tempestatis cantum putabant
and they thought their singing was the sighing of the storm

itaque cantus eorum nautis numquam pulchri sunt
therefore their songs were never beautiful to the sailors
quia si demersisset homines, demergeret
because if the ship sank the men would drown
de palatio Regis maris nihil lucrati sunt mortui
the dead gained nothing from the palace of the Sea King
sed soror eorum minima in fundo maris relicta
but their youngest sister was left at the bottom of the sea
Aspiciens autem eos, clamare paratus erat
looking up at them, she was ready to cry
scias Nereides lacrimas habere se posse flere
you should know mermaids have no tears that they can cry
sic dolor et aegritudo plus quam nostra fuit
so her pain and suffering was more acute than ours
"O utinam etiam quindecim annos natus essem!" dixit illa
"Oh, I wish I was also fifteen years old!" said she
"Scio quod illic mundum diligam".
"I know that I shall love the world up there"
"et diligam omnes homines qui habitant in hoc mundo".
"and I shall love all the people who live in that world"

Parva syreni natalis
The Little Mermaid's Birthday

at demum ipsa quoque ad quintum decimum diem natalem suum attigit
but, at last, she too reached her fifteenth birthday
"Avia" dixit "Avia"
"Well, now you are grown up," said her grandmother
"Veni, et ornem te sicut sorores tuae".
"Come, and let me adorn you like your sisters"
et imposuit sibi lilia candida crinem
And she placed a wreath of white lilies in her hair
omne folium liliorum dimidia margarita
every petal of the lilies was half a pearl
Tum vetula iussit octo magna ostrea venire
Then, the old lady ordered eight great oysters to come
ostreis se cauda reginae
the oysters attached themselves to the tail of the princess
sub mari ostrea sunt ostendere gradum
under the sea oysters are used to show your rank
"At ostrea ita mihi nocuerunt" dixit pusillus syreni
"But the oysters hurt me so," said the little mermaid
"Ita, scio ostrea laedere" respondit anicula
"Yes, I know oysters hurt," replied the old lady
"sed optime nosti quod superbia dolere debet".
"but you know very well that pride must suffer pain"
quam libenter omnem hanc magnificentiam exuisset!
how gladly she would have shaken off all this grandeur
amasset gravem deponere sertum!
she would have loved to lay aside the heavy wreath!
putavit de floribus rubris in horto suo
she thought of the red flowers in her own garden
flores rubri multo magis apti essent
the red flowers would have suited her much better
Sed in aliud se mutare non poterat
But she could not change herself into something else

sic vale dixit aviae et sororibus
so she said farewell to her grandmother and sisters
et, quam leviter bulla, in superficie surgit
and, as lightly as a bubble, she rose to the surface

Sol occiderat nuper, cum caput extulit undis
The sun had just set when she raised her head above the waves
Nubes cocco tinctae et auro ab occasu
The clouds were tinted with crimson and gold from the sunset
et sublustri eluxit ad vesperum
and through the glimmering twilight beamed the evening star
erat enim tranquillum mare, et erat aer lenis et recens
The sea was calm, and the sea air was mild and fresh
Navis magna cum tribus malis iacebat in aqua placide
A large ship with three masts lay lay calmly on the water
unum velum positum, non enim aura concitatur
only one sail was set, for not a breeze stirred
sedebant in navi vel inter armamenta nautae
and the sailors sat idle on deck, or amidst the rigging
Musica et carmina in nave erat
There was music and songs on board of the ship
sicut tenebrae centum lampadibus accensae sunt
as darkness came a hundred colored lanterns were lighted
quasi vexilla omnium gentium quassant in aere
it was as if the flags of all nations waved in the air

Parva syreni prope ad Cameram fenestrae natant
The little mermaid swam close to the cabin windows
interdum fluctus maris levavit eam
now and then the waves of the sea lifted her up
posset inspicere per fenestras vitreas
she could look in through the glass window-panes
et videre poterat multis curiose indutus hominibus
and she could see a number of curiously dressed people
Inter homines videre poterat Princeps iuvenis erat

Among the people she could see there was a young prince
Princeps pulcherrimus omnium
the prince was the most beautiful of them all
quae numquam viderat quis tam pulchros oculos
she had never seen anyone with such beautiful eyes
fuit celebratio sextus decimus natalis
it was the celebration of his sixteenth birthday
nautae in navi navis saltabant
The sailors were dancing on the deck of the ship
omnibus placuit cum princeps de Cameram
all cheered when the prince came out of the cabin
et plusquam centum nisl in aerem surrexerunt
and more than a hundred rockets rose into the air
aliquamdiu faces fecit caelum sicut splendor diei
for some time the fireworks made the sky as bright as day
certe noster iuvenis syreni pompam ante numquam viderat
of course our young mermaid had never seen fireworks before
commota omni voce, reversa est sub aquis
startled by all the noise, she went back under the water
mox iterum extendit caput
but soon she again stretched out her head
sicut omnia stellae caeli decidentes circa eam
it was as if all the stars of heaven were falling around her
splendidus sclopetis volavit in aerem caeruleum
splendid fireflies flew up into the blue air
omniaque in sereno tranquilloque relucent mari
and everything was reflected in the clear, calm sea
Navis ipsa luce ab omnibus illustrabatur
The ship itself was brightly illuminated by all the light
poterat videre omnes homines et vel minimum funem
she could see all the people and even the smallest rope
Quam formosus iuvenis gratias hospites aspexit!
How handsome the young prince looked thanking his guests!
et per noctem serena musica insonuit aura!
and the music resounded through the clear night air!

dies natalis serum noctis
the birthday celebrations lasted late into the night
at parva syreni oculos e navi auferre non potuit
but the little mermaid could not take her eyes from the ship
nec oculos a pulcro ducere posset
nor could she take her eyes from the beautiful prince
Colorata laternis iam exstincta
The colored lanterns had now been extinguished
nec plus nisl resurrexerunt in auras
and there were no more rockets that rose into the air
tormentum navis etiam incendere cessavit
the cannon of the ship had also ceased firing
nunc mare turbatum est
but now it was the sea that became restless
gemitus, murmure, sonitus, exaudiri sub undis
a moaning, grumbling sound could be heard beneath the waves
et tamen parva syreni per fenestram Cameram manebat
and yet, the little mermaid remained by the cabin window
illa gestatio et descendit super aquam
she was rocking up and down on the water
ut inspicere posset navem
so that she could keep looking into the ship
Post aliquantum vela celeriter profecti
After a while the sails were quickly set
et ivit navis iter ad portum
and the ship went on her way back to port

Sed mox altiores et altiores undae
But soon the waves rose higher and higher
obscurum, gravia nubila caelum
dark, heavy clouds darkened the night sky
et apparuerunt fulgura in distantia
and there appeared flashes of lightning in the distance
haud procul ingens tempestas aderat
not far away a dreadful storm was approaching

Vela iterum demissa contra ventum
Once more the sails were lowered against the wind
et magna ratis fugientem perstitit aequor
and the great ship pursued her course over the raging sea
Fluctus usque ad montes surrexerunt
The waves rose as high as the mountains
putares undas navis habituras
one would have thought the waves were going to have the ship
sed navis quasi cycni inter undas iacitur
but the ship dived like a swan between the waves
tum resurrexit ab altis, Spumantibus cristis
then she rose again on their lofty, foaming crests
Parvulo syreni hoc pulchrum spectaculum fuit
To the little mermaid this was pleasant to watch
sed non erat jucundum nautis
but it was not pleasant for the sailors
navis ingemens et stridens fecit
the ship made awful groaning and creaking sounds
et iterum atque iterum fluctus super navi texuit
and the waves broke over the deck of the ship again and again
densissima tignis cessit sub uerbera maris
the thick planks gave way under the lashing of the sea
cogente principali dirupta sicut arundo
under the pressure the mainmast snapped asunder, like a reed
et, dum navis in latere iacebat, aqua irruit
and, as the ship lay over on her side, the water rushed in

Parva syreni turbam in periculo esse intellexit
The little mermaid realized that the crew were in danger
sui rei non sine periculo vel
her own situation wasn't without danger either
tigna et asseres sparsos vitare per undas
she had to avoid the beams and planks scattered in the water
paulisper versa est in meras tenebras
for a moment everything turned into complete darkness

et parva syreni non poterat videre ubi esset
and the little mermaid could not see where she was
sed tunc fulgur coruscans totam scenam revelavit
but then a flash of lightning revealed the whole scene
omnes videre poterat adhuc in nave
she could see everyone was still on board of the ship
bene omnes in navi erant, praeter principem;
well, everyone was on board of the ship, except the prince
Prosequebatur navis iter ad terram
the ship continued on its path to the land
et vidit in alto mergi principem
and she saw the prince sink into the deep waves
hoc momento feliciorem fecit
for a moment this made her happier than it should have
nunc cum in mari posset esse cum eo
now that he was in the sea she could be with him
Tum limites hominum recordata est
Then she remembered the limits of human beings
terra autem populus non vivet in aqua
the people of the land cannot live in the water
si ad regiam pervenisset, iam mortuus esset
if he got to the palace he would already be dead
"Minime, non debet mori!" quae placuit
"No, he must not die!" she decided
non oblivisci aliquam sollicitudinem pro salute sua
she forget any concern for her own safety
et transnatat per tigna et asseres
and she swam through the beams and planks
duas trabes facile comminuet eam
two beams could easily crush her to pieces
columbæ alta sub tenebris aquis
she dove deep under the dark waters
Omnia surgens fluctu
everything rose and fell with the waves
tandem assequendum iuvenem principem
finally, she managed to reach the young prince

ieiunus erat amissa potentia natandi in mare turbidum
he was fast losing the power to swim in the stormy sea
Membra eius deficere incipiebant
His limbs were starting to fail him
et clausis oculis pulchris
and his beautiful eyes were closed
mortuus esset si parva syreni veniret
he would have died had the little mermaid not come
Illa tenebat caput super aquam
She held his head above the water
et illa, qua volebant, fluctus portaret
and she let the waves carry them where they wanted

Mane tempestas cessavit
In the morning the storm had ceased
sed navis ne fragmentum quidem videri poterat
but of the ship not a single fragment could be seen
Ascendit sol, rutilans et lucens ab aqua
The sun came up, red and shining, out of the water
solis radiis princeps effectus medentis
the sun's beams had a healing effect on the prince
color sanitatis ad genas principis rediit
the hue of health returned to the prince's cheeks
sed non obstante sole, clausis oculis
but despite the sun, his eyes remained closed
Suam osculatus est altam, laevi frontem
The mermaid kissed his high, smooth forehead
et permulsit madidas comas
and she stroked back his wet hair
Marmoreo ei videbatur in horto suo
He seemed to her like the marble statue in her garden
Et iterum osculata est eum, et volebat vivere
so she kissed him again, and wished that he lived

Et mox in conspectum terre venerunt
Presently, they came in sight of land

et vidit caeruleos altos montes in horizonte
and she saw lofty blue mountains on the horizon
super montes alba nix quievit
on top of the mountains the white snow rested
quasi grex olorum in montibus iacebat
as if a flock of swans were lying upon the mountains
Silvae virides pulchrae prope litus erant
Beautiful green forests were near the shore
et iuxta eum stabat aedificium magnum
and close by there stood a large building
posset esse ecclesia vel conventus
it could have been a church or a convent
sed etiam longe fuit ut fideles
but she was still too far away to be sure
Aurei et citreae arbores in horto creverunt
Orange and citron trees grew in the garden
et ante ostium palmae altae steterunt
and before the door stood lofty palms
Mare parvus sinus
The sea here formed a little bay
in sinu aqua quievit et adhuc
in the bay the water lay quiet and still
sed adhuc aqua erat valde profunda
but although the water was still, it was very deep
Natavit cum decorum princeps ad litus
She swam with the handsome prince to the beach
litore texit bysso alba harenae
the beach was covered with fine white sand
et super harenam posuit eum in sole calido
and on the sand she laid him in the warm sunshine
erigere caput altius quam corpus curabat
she took care to raise his head higher than his body
Tunc campanae sonuerunt ex magna aedificio albo
Then bells sounded from the large white building
nonnullae puellae in hortum venerunt
some young girls came into the garden

Longius e litore natavit Syre- nus
The little mermaid swam out farther from the shore
in altissimis saxis se abdidit aquis
she hid herself among some high rocks in the water
operuit caput et collum spuma maris
she covered her head and neck with the foam of the sea
et observabat videre quid principi pauperi accideret
and she watched to see what would become of the poor prince

Non multo ante vidit puellam appropinquare
It was not long before she saw a young girl approach
puella videbatur territus primo
the young girl seemed frightened, at first
sed timor tantum momento duravit
but her fear only lasted for a moment
tum traductis multis
then she brought over a number of people
et vidit Syrena quod revixit princeps
and the mermaid saw that the prince came to life again
subridens his qui circumsteterunt eum
he smiled upon those who stood around him
Sed paulo risus principe nulla syreni
But to the little mermaid the prince sent no smile
nesciebat enim quod ipsa esset quae eum servasset
he knew not that it was her who had saved him
Hoc pusillum syreni nimis tristem fecit
This made the little mermaid very sorrowful
et inde ad magnum aedificium abductus est
and then he was led away into the great building
et pusillus syreni iactus in aquam
and the little mermaid dived down into the water
et reversa est ad castrum patris sui
and she returned to her father's castle

In Parva syreni desideria superioris mundi
The Little Mermaid Longs for the Upper World

Illa semper tacitissima et cogitata sororum fuerat
She had always been the most silent and thoughtful of the sisters
et nunc magis tacita et cogitata magis quam semper fuit
and now she was more silent and thoughtful than ever
Interrogaverunt eam sorores eius, quid vidisset in primo adventu eius
Her sisters asked her what she had seen on her first visit
sed nihil eorum quae viderat poterat dicere
but she could tell them nothing of what she had seen
Multa vespere et mane rediit ad superficiem
Many an evening and morning she returned to the surface
et ivit ad locum ubi exierat princeps
and she went to the place where she had left the prince
Fructus in horto vidit
She saw the fruits in the garden ripen
et vidit fructus ex arboribus suis collectos
and she watched the fruits gathered from their trees
Vidit nix in montibus tabescere
she watched the snow on the mountain tops melt away
sed in nulla visitatione sua principem adhuc vidit
but on none of her visits did she see the prince again
ideoque semper tristior reversa est quam illa excessit
and therefore she always returned more sorrowful than when she left

ea sola consolatio sedebat in hortulo suo
her only comfort was sitting in her own little garden
bracchia circum pulchra marmorea
she flung her arms around the beautiful marble statue
statuam quae vidi sicut princeps
the statue which looked just like the prince
Flores suos tendens in eam dederat

She had given up tending to her flowers
et hortus eius creverunt in confusione silvestrium
and her garden grew in wild confusion
longa folia et caules florum circum arborum texebant
they twinied the long leaves and stems of the flowers around the trees
ita ut totus hortus tenebrosus et maesus factus sit
so that the whole garden became dark and gloomy

tandem ferre dolorem non
eventually she could bear the pain no longer
et narravit uni sororum suarum omnia quae contigerant
and she told one of her sisters all that had happened
mox aliae sorores audiverunt secretum
soon the other sisters heard the secret
Et mox occultum eius pluribus puellis innotuit
and very soon her secret became known to several maids
unus ex ancillis amicus erat qui noverat de principe
one of the maids had a friend who knew about the prince
Illa etiam festum in nave vidisset
She had also seen the festival on board the ship
et dixit eis unde princeps venit
and she told them where the prince came from
et indicavit eis ubi stabat palatium suum
and she told them where his palace stood

"Veni, soror, parva", inquit ceterae reginae
"Come, little sister," said the other princesses
nexa armis consurgunt
they entwined their arms and rose up together
perrexerunt ad palatium principis
they went near to where the prince's palace stood
palatium ex fulvo et nitido lapide aedificatum est
the palace was built of bright-yellow, shining stone
et regia longa volatus marmorei vestigia
and the palace had long flights of marble steps

unus de gradibus volatus usque ad mare pervenit
one of the flights of steps reached down to the sea
Splendide aurata cupolas super tecta levavit
Splendid gilded cupolas rose over the roof
totum aedificium columnis cingebatur
the whole building was surrounded by pillars
et inter columnas stabant statuae marmoreae ad vivum
and between the pillars stood lifelike statues of marble
per clarum cristallum fenestras viderent
they could see through the clear crystal of the windows
et inspicere possent nobilia cubicula
and they could look into the noble rooms
aulaea pretiosa et aulaea e lacunari setis pendentibus
costly silk curtains and tapestries hung from the ceiling
et parietes picturis pulchris tegebant
and the walls were covered with beautiful paintings
In medio maximi Salon erat fons
In the centre of the largest salon was a fountain
fons scintillans rumpit alte
the fountain threw its sparkling jets high up
spargitur aqua super vitrum cupola laquearia
the water splashed onto the glass cupola of the ceiling
et sol lucebat per aquam
and the sun shone in through the water
et in plantis circa fontem aqua spargitur
and the water splashed on the plants around the fountain

Nunc parvula syreni sciebat ubi princeps habitabat
Now the little mermaid knew where the prince lived
ita multam noctem in illis aquis
so she spent many a night in those waters
fortius obtinuit eam sororibus eius quam fuerat
she got more courageous than her sisters had been
et litora multo propiora natant
and she swam much nearer the shore than they had
quondam alveum angustum ascendit, sub podio marmoreo

once she went up the narrow channel, under the marble balcony
SOLARIUM umbram latam super aquam
the balcony threw a broad shadow on the water
Hic sedit et vidit principem iuvenem
Here she sat and watched the young prince
Ille nimirum solus in luce lunae putabat
he, of course, thought he was alone in the bright moonlight

Saepe vidit eum ad vesperas in navi pulchra navigantem
She often saw him in the evenings, sailing in a beautiful boat
musica e navi et vexillis agitantibus cecinit
music sounded from the boat and the flags waved
Aglauros viridis e iunco
She peeped out from among the green rushes
interdum longam vento tenuit argenteo velam
at times the wind caught her long silvery-white veil
qui velum eius viderunt cygnum esse credebant
those who saw her veil believed it to be a swan
velamen omne cycni specie pennae patulae
her veil had all the appearance of a swan spreading its wings

Multa nocte etiam speculator piscatores retia posuerunt
Many a night, too, she watched the fishermen set their nets
retia in luce faces
they cast their nets in the light of their torches
et audiuit eos de principe multa bona dicere
and she heard them tell many good things about the prince
hoc laetatum est quod vitam suam conservaverat
this made her glad that she had saved his life
quando circa medium iactatus undis
when he was tossed around half dead on the waves
Recordata est quomodo caput eius in sinu eius requieverat
She remembered how his head had rested on her bosom
et recordata est quam ex animo osculatus est eum
and she remembered how heartily she had kissed him

sed omnia, quae acciderant, nihil sciebat
but he knew nothing of all that had happened
adulescens ne somnium quidem parva syreni
the young prince could not even dream of the little mermaid

Crevit ut homines magis ac magis
She grew to like human beings more and more
magis magisque vellet suum mundum vagari posse
she wished more and more to be able to wander their world
orbis eorum videbatur esse tam maior quam sua
their world seemed to be so much larger than her own
In navibus trans mare volitabant
They could fly over the sea in ships
et summos montes conscendere longe supra nubila
and they could mount the high hills far above the clouds
in eorum agris silvas et agros possederunt
in their lands they possessed woods and fields
viror extenditur ultra aspectum
the greenery stretched beyond the reach of her sight
Tantum erat ut scire vellet!
There was so much that she wished to know!
sed sorores eius non poterant respondere ad omnes quaestiones
but her sisters were unable to answer all her questions
Tum ad senem aviam responsa
She then went to her old grandmother for answers
aviam sciebant omnes superiores
her grandmother knew all about the upper world
recte hunc mundum "terras super mare" appellavit.
she rightly called this world "the lands above the sea"

"Si non submerguntur homines, possuntne vivere in aeternum?"
"If human beings are not drowned, can they live forever?"
"Numquamne morimur, sicut hic in mari facimus?"
"Do they never die, as we do here in the sea?"

"Ita, etiam moriuntur", respondit anus
"Yes, they die too," replied the old lady
"similis nobis quoque moriendum" addidit aviam
"like us, they must also die," added her grandmother
et vita eorum brevior est quam nostra.
"and their lives are even shorter than ours"
"Nonnumquam trecentis annis vivimus"
"We sometimes live for three hundred years"
"sed cum hic esse desinimus, spumas fiamus".
"but when we cease to exist here we become foam"
"Et aquae supernatet"
"and we float on the surface of the water"
" monumenta non habemus illis quos amamus "
"we do not have graves for those we love"
et non habemus animas immortales.
"and we have not immortal souls"
"Postquam moriemur numquam reviviscimus"
"after we die we shall never live again"
"sicut viridis alga, semel excisa".
"like the green seaweed, once it has been cut off"
"Postquam morimur, numquam iterum reflorescere possumus".
"after we die, we can never flourish again"
Homines autem habent animas.
"Human beings, on the contrary, have souls"
"Etiam postquam mortuus es, anima eorum in aeternum vive".
"even after they're dead their souls live forever"
" cum morimur corpora nostra in spumam vertere " .
"when we die our bodies turn to foam"
"cum moriuntur corpora in pulverem"
"when they die their bodies turn to dust"
"cum morimur, per claram caerula aquam surgimus".
"when we die we rise through the clear, blue water"
"cum per purum purum consurgitur auras".
"when they die they rise up through the clear, pure air"

"Cum morimur, nihil ultra quam superficies natamus"
"when we die we float no further than the surface"
"sed cum moriuntur, micant supergrediuntur sidera".
"but when they die they go beyond the glittering stars"
"Ex aqua ad superficiem surgimus"
"we rise out of the water to the surface"
"et uidemus omnem terram"
"and we behold all the land of the earth"
"Ad ignotas et gloriosas regiones surgunt"
"they rise to unknown and glorious regions"
" Gloriosas et ignotas regiones quas numquam videbimus " ;
"glorious and unknown regions which we shall never see"
parum syreni doluerunt animae indigentiam
the little mermaid mourned her lack of a soul
"Cur non habemus animas immortales?" rogavit paulo syreni
"Why have not we immortal souls?" asked the little mermaid
"Libenter omnibus centenis annis quod habeo dare"
"I would gladly give all the hundreds of years that I have"
"Me trado totum esse hominem in unum diem".
"I would trade it all to be a human being for one day"
"Non possum existimare spem talem cognoscendi felicitatem";
"I can not imagine the hope of knowing such happiness"
" felicitas mundi gloriosi super astra "
"the happiness of that glorious world above the stars"
"Non modo putes" dixit anus
"You must not think that way," said the old woman
"Credimus nos multo feliciores esse hominibus"
"We believe that we are much happier than the humans"
" et credimus nos multo meliores esse quam homines "
"and we believe we are much better off than human beings"

"Sic moriar", inquit parvus syreni
"So I shall die," said the little mermaid
spuma maris cum lavetur";
"being the foam of the sea, I shall be washed about"

"Nunquam iterum musicam fluctuum audio".
"never again will I hear the music of the waves"
"Numquam iterum videbo satis flores"
"never again will I see the pretty flowers"
"Nec me visurus rursus Solem rubrum".
"nor will I ever again see the red sun"
"Numquid possum immortalem animam impetrare?"
"Is there anything I can do to win an immortal soul?"
"Minime," inquit anus, "nisi..."
"No," said the old woman, "unless..."
"unus est modus lucrandi animam"
"there is just one way to gain a soul"
"Homo te plus diligit quam patrem et matrem".
"a man has to love you more than he loves his father and mother"
"Omnes cogitationes eius et amor in te fixa sunt".
"all his thoughts and love must be fixed upon you"
"Promittere debet verum esse tibi hic et posthac".
"he has to promise to be true to you here and hereafter"
"sacerdos dextram tuam in te ponere debet".
"the priest has to place his right hand in yours"
"anima ergo hominis tui labatur in corpus tuum";
"then your man's soul would glide into your body"
"Vobis participationem futurae beatitudinis hominum"
"you would get a share in the future happiness of mankind"
"Dat tibi animam, et propriam retineat".
"He would give to you a soul and retain his own as well"
sed impossibile est hoc semper evenire.
"but it is impossible for this to ever happen"
"Cauda piscis tui apud nos formosa habetur".
"Your fish's tail, among us, is considered beautiful"
"sed in terris piscis cauda turpis habetur".
"but on earth your fish's tail is considered ugly"
"homines melius non norunt"
"The humans do not know any better"
"Vexillum pulchritudinis est habens duo fulcra"

"their standard of beauty is having two stout props"
"hi duo fulcra vocant crura";
"these two stout props they call their legs"
Ingemuit parvula syreni quod fatum eius esse videbatur
The little mermaid sighed at what appeared to be her destiny
et aspexit maerens ad caudam piscis
and she looked sorrowfully at her fish's tail
"Laetemus quod habemus" dixit anicula
"Let us be happy with what we have," said the old lady
" Tercentum feremus annos spicula nobis " .
"let us dart and spring about for the three hundred years"
"et trecentos annos vere satis diu est"
"and three hundred years really is quite long enough"
"Post hoc melius nosmet ipsos quiescere possumus";
"After that we can rest ourselves all the better"
"Hoc vespere pilam atrium habiturum sumus"
"This evening we are going to have a court ball"

Is fuit unus ex illis quae praeclaris aspectibus in terris videre numquam possumus
It was one of those splendid sights we can never see on earth
et atrium pila tulit in magna ballroom
the court ball took place in a large ballroom
Muri et laquearia erant spissa cristallo pellucentia
The walls and the ceiling were of thick transparent crystal
Multa centena perampla maris conchae steterunt in utroque latere ordines
Many hundreds of colossal sea shells stood in rows on each side
Conchae marinae aliae rubrae, aliae herbae virides
some of the sea shells were deep red, others were grass green
et singula conchis marinis ignem caeruleum habebat
and each of the sea shells had a blue fire in it
Ignes hi totum Salonem et saltatores accenderunt
These fires lighted up the whole salon and the dancers
et concha per parietes refulserunt

and the sea shells shone out through the walls
ita ut mare etiam luce sua inluminetur
so that the sea was also illuminated by their light
Pisces innumerabiles maiores et minores nataverunt
Innumerable fishes, great and small, swam past
quidam ex piscibus squamae purpureo fulgore incanduerunt
some of the fishes scales glowed with a purple brilliance
et alii pisces fulgebant argento et auro
and other fishes shone like silver and gold
atria lata per amnis ibat
Through the halls flowed a broad stream
et in rivo saltaverunt nereii et nerei
and in the stream danced the mermen and the mermaids
ad musicam suam dulcem cantilenam saltabant
they danced to the music of their own sweet singing

Nemo in terra tam pulchras voces habet quam hi
No one on earth has such lovely voices as they
sed homunculus syreni dulcius omnibus cantabat
but the little mermaid sang more sweetly than all
Tota curia plaudit eam manibus et caudis
The whole court applauded her with hands and tails
et in tempore suo cor sensit satis felix
and for a moment her heart felt quite happy
quia sciebat eam vocem dulcissimam habere in mari
because she knew she had the sweetest voice in the sea
et sciret vocem dulcissimam habere in terra
and she knew she had the sweetest voice on land
Moxque iterum mundi supera putavit
But soon she thought again of the world above her
oblivisci non poterat princeps venuste
she could not forget the charming prince
recordatus est ei se habere animam immortalem
it reminded her that he had an immortal soul
et oblivisci non poterat se nullam habere animam immortalem

and she could not forget that she had no immortal soul
tacite irrepsit e palatio patris
She crept away silently out of her father's palace
omnia intus plena laetitia et cantu
everything within was full of gladness and song
sed sedit in suo hortulo, moestus et solus
but she sat in her own little garden, sorrowful and alone
Tunc audivit tubam per aquam sonantem
Then she heard the bugle sounding through the water
et putavit " Ipse navigat ";
and she thought, "He is certainly sailing above"
"Princeps pulcherrimus, in quo mea vota media".
"he, the beautiful prince, in whom my wishes centre"
"Ille, in cuius manibus felicitatem meam collocare uelim".
"he, in whose hands I should like to place my happiness"
" Audebo omnes immortalem sibi conciliare animam ".
"I will venture all for him to win an immortal soul"
" Sorores meae in palatio patris mei saltant ".
"my sisters are dancing in my father's palace"
"sed ibo ad mare maga"
"but I will go to the sea witch"
" maga marina de qua semper tam timui ".
"the sea witch of whom I have always been so afraid"
"sed maga marina mihi consilium potest dare et auxilium"
"but the sea witch can give me counsel, and help"

Mare Maga
The Sea Witch

Tunc exivit de hortulo suo pusilla
Then the little mermaid went out from her garden
et iter ad spumas ducebat ad undas
and she took the path to the foaming whirlpools
post spumosi voragines maga fuit
behind the foaming whirlpools the sorceress lived
numquam illuc ante syreni
the little mermaid had never gone that way before
neque flores neque gramen quo ibat creverunt
Neither flowers nor grass grew where she was going
nihil nisi nudum, cinereum, arenosum
there was nothing but bare, gray, sandy ground
haec terra sterilis extendit ad voraginem
this barren land stretched out to the whirlpool
aqua quasi spumans molendini rotarum
the water was like foaming mill wheels
et gurges omnibua introeuntibus
and the whirlpools seized everything that came within reach
voragines praedam in profundo
the whirlpools cast their prey into the fathomless deep
Per hos voragines opprimendi oportuit transire
Through these crushing whirlpools she had to pass
tunc demum potuit maga ditione maris attingere
only then could she reach the dominions of the sea witch
postea calido, luto bulliente
after this came a stretch of warm, bubbling mire
maga marina dicitur caespite iunci glaucaque paludis
the sea witch called the bubbling mire her turf moor

Ultra caespitem mora fuit maga in domo
Beyond her turf moor was the witch's house
domus eius stetit in medio silvae alienae
her house stood in the centre of a strange forest

In hac silva omnes arbores et flores polypi erant
in this forest all the trees and flowers were polypi
sed erant semivivi tantum; alterum medium est animal
but they were only half plant; the other half was animal
Centum capitibus erant sicut serpentes
They looked like serpents with a hundred heads
et crescebat unusquisque serpens de terra
and each serpent was growing out of the ground
Rami longi, lacerti leves
Their branches were long, slimy arms
habebantque digitos quasi vermes flexibiles
and they had fingers like flexible worms
singula membra, a radice usque ad summum
each of their limbs, from the root to the top, moved
Omnia quae in mari potuerunt pervenerunt
All that could be reached in the sea they seized upon
et quod ceperunt arcte tenuerunt
and what they caught they held on tightly to
ut, quod prensi sunt, numquam ex manibus evaserint
so that what they caught never escaped from their clutches

Parvula syreni pertimuit quod vidit
The little mermaid was alarmed at what she saw
et stetisset in corde pavore
she stood still and her heart beat with fear
Proxima ad conversionem venit
She came very close to turning back
sed putavit principis pulcherrimi
but she thought of the beautiful prince
et de anima humana, pro qua cupiebat, cogitavit
and she thought of the human soul for which she longed
his cogitationibus virtus rediit
with these thoughts her courage returned
defixit promissos crines circum caput
She fastened her long, flowing hair round her head
ut polypi capillum tenere non posset

so that the polypi could not grab hold of her hair
et traiecit manus suas per sinum suum
and she crossed her hands across her bosom
et tunc transvolavit sicut pisces per aquam
and then she darted forward like a fish through the water
inter brachia subtilia digitosque deformis polypi
between the subtle arms and fingers of the ugly polypi
polypi ex utraque parte eius extendebantur
the polypi were stretched out on each side of her
Vidit omnes aliquid in manibus tenere
She saw that they all held something in their grasp
quod multis armis occupaverant
something they had seized with their numerous little arms
qui tenebant alba sceleta hominum
they were holding white skeletons of human beings
nautae qui in procellis mari perierunt
sailors who had perished at sea in storms
nautae qui in altas delapsi sunt
sailors who had sunk down into the deep waters
et sceleta terrenorum erant
and there were skeletons of land animals
et remi, clavos, et pectora navium
and there were oars, rudders, and chests of ships
Erat etiam pusillus syrenus, quem ceperant
There was even a little mermaid whom they had caught
pauper Syreni manibus strangulatus est
the poor mermaid must have been strangled by the hands
ei haec omnia foedissima videbantur
to her this seemed the most shocking of all

tandem ad spatium palustri in silvis
finally, she came to a space of marshy ground in the woods
Hic erant multae aquae pingues serpentes in luto volventes
here there were large fat water snakes rolling in the mire
serpentes monstrent sua corpora foeda, moecha, pulla
the snakes showed their ugly, drab-colored bodies

In medio hujus loci stabat domus
In the midst of this spot stood a house
domus ex ossibus hominum naufragorum aedificata est
the house was built of the bones of shipwrecked human beings
et in domo sedit mare maga
and in the house sat the sea witch
illa permittens bufonem edere de ore eius
she was allowing a toad to eat from her mouth
sicut cum populus pascat Canarias frusta saccharo
just like when people feed a canary with pieces of sugar
Aquae foedae serpentes pullos suos appellabat
She called the ugly water snakes her little chickens
Et permisit sibi pullos suos super totum serpere
and she allowed her little chickens to crawl all over her

"Scio quid vis," dixit maga marina
"I know what you want," said the sea witch
"Stultum est de vobis tale aliquid velle".
"It is very stupid of you to want such a thing"
"sed habebis viam, quamlibet stulta est".
"but you shall have your way, however stupid it is"
"Quamquam voluntas tua te ad tristitiam feret, mea bella regina".
"though your wish will bring you to sorrow, my pretty princess"
"Tu vellere caudam syreni tui"
"You want to get rid of your mermaid's tail"
"et habere vis duas stirpes loco"
"and you want to have two stumps instead"
"Hoc te faciet sicut homines in terra".
"this will make you like the human beings on earth"
"Et tunc in amorem incidere cum princeps iuvenis tecum"
"and then the young prince might fall in love with you"
"et tunc haberes animam immortalem".
"and then you might have an immortal soul"

maga risit et turpiter
the witch laughed loud and disgustingly
bufo et serpentes corruerunt in terram
the toad and the snakes fell to the ground
et ponunt ibi luctantes humi
and they lay there wriggling on the floor
"Maleficus ad me venisti" dixit
"You came to me just in time," said the witch
"Post solis ortum cras sera fuisset"
"after sunrise tomorrow it would have been too late"
"Post crastinum non potui adiuvare vos usque ad finem alterius anni".
"after tomorrow I would not have been able to help you till the end of another year"
"Potionem parabo tibi"
"I will prepare a potion for you"
"Ad terram natare cras ante solis ortum"
"swim up to the land tomorrow, before sunrise"
ibi sede te, et bibe potionem;
"seat yourself there and drink the potion"
"Postquam biberis potio caudam tuam abibit"
"after you drink the potion your tail will disappear"
" tum habebis quod vocant pedes "
"and then you will have what men call legs"

"Omnes dicent te pulcherrima puella in mundo"
"all will say you are the prettiest girl in the world"
" sed propter hoc magnum erit perferre dolorem " .
"but for this you will have to endure great pain"
"sicut gladius per te transiret".
"it will be as if a sword were passing through you"
" Adhuc idem habebis motus venustatis " ;
"You will still have the same gracefulness of movement"
"erit quasi super humum innatans"
"it will be as if you are floating over the ground"
"et saltator non umquam calcabit quam tu"

"and no dancer will ever tread as lightly as you"
"sed omnem gradum quem ceperis magnum dolorem faciam tibi"
"but every step you take will cause you great pain"
"erit quasi cultris acutis calcans".
"it will be as if you were treading upon sharp knives"
"Si feres omnem hunc dolorem, adiuvabo te".
"If you bear all this suffering, I will help you"
pusillum syreni cogitationis principis
the little mermaid thought of the prince
et felicitatem animae immortalis putavit
and she thought of the happiness of an immortal soul
"Ita, volo," dixit parva regina
"Yes, I will," said the little princess
sed, ut credis, vox tremit
but, as you can imagine, her voice trembled with fear

"Noli in hunc irruere" dixit maga
"do not rush into this," said the witch
"quondam homo conformatus es, numquam redire potes"
"once you are shaped like a human, you can never return"
"et numquam iterum formam syreni".
"and you will never again take the form of a mermaid"
"Per aquam sororibus tuis numquam redibis".
"You will never return through the water to your sisters"
"nec umquam ad palatium patris tui iterum ibis".
"nor will you ever go to your father's palace again"
" Habebis amorem principis conciliare ".
"you will have to win the love of the prince"
" debet oblivisci tui patris et matris tuae ".
"he must be willing to forget his father and mother for you"
"et debet diligere te ex tota anima sua".
"and he must love you with all of his soul"
"sacerdos manus tuas debet copulare".
"the priest must join your hands together"
"et in sacro matrimonio faciat te virum et uxorem".

"and he must make you man and wife in holy matrimony"
"Tantum ergo habebis animam immortalem"
"only then will you have an immortal soul"
"sed tu numquam permittas eum alteri mulieri nubere"
"but you must never allow him to marry another woman"
"Mane postquam aliam uxorem ducit, cor tuum confringet".
"the morning after he marries another woman, your heart will break"
"et fies spumas in summis fluctibus".
"and you will become foam on the crest of the waves"
pusillus syreni factus est sicut mors pallida
the little mermaid became as pale as death
"Faciam," inquit pusillus syreni
"I will do it," said the little mermaid

"Sed solvendum etiam est," dixit maleficus
"But I must be paid, also," said the witch
et parum est quod peto.
"and it is not a trifle that I ask for"
"Vox suavissima habes hic habitantium"
"You have the sweetest voice of any who dwell here"
" Principem voce tua delectare te posse credis "
"you believe that you can charm the prince with your voice"
"Sed vocem pulchram tuam mihi dare debes".
"But your beautiful voice you must give to me"
"Melimum quod possides, potionis meae pretium est".
"The best thing you possess is the price of my potion"
"Potio sanguine meo miscenda est"
"the potion must be mixed with my own blood"
"sola haec mixtura potionem facit tam acuta quam gladius biceps"
"only this mixture makes the potion as sharp as a two-edged sword"

parva syreni conatus recusare sumptus
the little mermaid tried to object to the cost

"At si vocem meam aufers..." dixit pusillus syreni
"But if you take away my voice..." said the little mermaid
"Si vocem meam aufers, quid mihi restat?"
"if you take away my voice, what is left for me?"
"formam pulchram tuam" maga suggessit mare
"Your beautiful form," suggested the sea witch
"gratia tua ambula, et oculi tui expressi".
"your graceful walk, and your expressive eyes"
"Numquid his rebus cor hominis extorquere potes?"
"Surely, with these things you can enchain a man's heart?"
"Age, perdidisti animum tuum?" maris pythonissam petivit
"Well, have you lost your courage?" the sea witch asked
"Extende linguam tuam, ut eam exscindam".
"Put out your little tongue, so that I can cut it off"
tunc potio potens erit.
"then you shall have the powerful potion"
"Fiet," inquit parvus syreni
"It shall be," said the little mermaid

Tum maga ahenum in ignem posuit
Then the witch placed her cauldron on the fire
"Munitas est bona res", dixit maga marina
"Cleanliness is a good thing," said the sea witch
defricans vasa ius anguis
she scoured the vessels for the right snake
omnes angues magno nodo colligati
all the snakes had been tied together in a large knot
Tum compunctus ad pectus
Then she pricked herself in the breast
et mittat sanguinem nigrum in lebetem
and she let the black blood drop into the caldron
Vapor qui rosa se torquet in horrendas figuras
The steam that rose twisted itself into horrible shapes
nemo poterat intueri formas sine timore
no person could look at the shapes without fear
Quovis momento maga nova ingredientia in vas projecit

Every moment the witch threw new ingredients into the vessel
postremo, omnibus intus rebus, coquere lebetem
finally, with everything inside, the caldron began to boil
sonus erat quasi fletus crocodili
there was the sound like the weeping of a crocodile
et tandem potio magica parata erat
and at last the magic potion was ready
potio non obstante ejus ingredientia, visi sunt sicut aqua lucidissima
despite its ingredients, the potion looked like the clearest water
"Ibi est, omnia tibi," dixit maleficus
"There it is, all for you," said the witch
et tunc abscidit linguas vernulas
and then she cut off the little mermaid's tongue
ita ut numquam adhuc pusillus syre- nae loquatur neque iterum canat
so that the little mermaid could never again speak, nor sing again
"Polypi temptare atque capto in exitum"
"the polypi might try and grab you on the way out"
si conantur, paucas guttas potionis super eos mittite.
"if they try, throw over them a few drops of the potion"
et digiti eorum discerpentur in mille partes.
"and their fingers will be torn into a thousand pieces"
Sed parva syreni hoc facere non oportebat
But the little mermaid had no need to do this
Polypi trepidi recesserunt cum viderunt illam
the polypi sprang back in terror when they saw her
ut vidit eam amisisse magam linguam ad mare
they saw she had lost her tongue to the sea witch
et viderunt illam potionem portantem
and they saw she was carrying the potion
et potio fulgebat in manu eius sicut stella
the potion shone in her hand like a twinkling star

Transivit ergo cito per silvam et paludem
So she passed quickly through the wood and the marsh
et transiit inter rapidas gurgites
and she passed between the rushing whirlpools
mox rediit ad palatium patris sui
soon she made her way back to the palace of her father
omnes faces in ballroom exstincta sunt
all the torches in the ballroom were extinguished
nunc omnes intra palatium dormientes
all within the palace must now be asleep
Sed non intrabat ad eos
But she did not go inside to see them
scivit eam in perpetuum exiturus
she knew she was going to leave them forever
et sciebat cor eius, si videret
and she knew her heart would break if she saw them
et abiit in hortum unum extremum tempus
she went into the garden one last time
et sumpsit florem ex unaquaque sororum suarum
and she took a flower from each one of her sisters
et tunc surrexit per aquas caeruleas
and then she rose up through the dark-blue waters

Parva syreni Principis in Meets
The Little Mermaid Meets the Prince

parva syreni principis palatium pervenit
the little mermaid arrived at the prince's palace
nondum sol ortus erat
the sun had not yet risen from the sea
et luna splendens et clara in nocte
and the moon shone clear and bright in the night
parum syreni sedit ad vestigia pulchra marmorea
the little mermaid sat at the beautiful marble steps
potionem magicam bibit et pusillus syreni
and then the little mermaid drank the magic potion
sensit incisionem ancipiti gladio incidi per eam
she felt the cut of a two-edged sword cut through her
et incidit in deliquium et incubuit sicut mortuus
and she fell into a swoon, and lay like one dead
sol exortus est de mari et refulsit super terram
the sun rose from the sea and shone over the land
convaluit et sensit dolorem de sectis
she recovered and felt the pain from the cut
sed ante eam stabat pulcher iuvenis princeps
but before her stood the handsome young prince

Oculos suos carbonum nigros in pusillum syreni infixit
He fixed his coal-black eyes upon the little mermaid
aspexit vehementer ut oculos deiecit
he looked so earnestly that she cast down her eyes
et tunc sensit caudam piscis illius abiisse
and then she became aware that her fish's tail was gone
Vidit se pulcherrimum par cruribus albis
she saw that she had the prettiest pair of white legs
et habebat parvos pedes, sicut aliqua puella
and she had tiny feet, as any little maiden would have
Sed cum de mari venisset, vestimenta sua non habuit
But, having come from the sea, she had no clothes

sic involvit se longo et crasso capillo
so she wrapped herself in her long, thick hair
Princeps interrogavit eam quaenam esset et unde
The prince asked her who she was and whence she came
Aspexit eum clementer et dolens
She looked at him mildly and sorrowfully
sed quod responderet oculis caeruleis
but she had to answer with her deep blue eyes
quia parva syreni amplius loqui non potuit
because the little mermaid could not speak anymore
Et apprehensa manu eius , adduxit eam in palatium
He took her by the hand and led her to the palace

Omnis gradus sumpsit erat, sicut maga dixerat fore
Every step she took was as the witch had said it would be
sensit ac si cultros calcabat acutos
she felt as if she were treading upon sharp knives
Dolorem velit velit, autem
She bore the pain of her wish willingly, however
et movit ad latus principis leviter quasi bulla
and she moved at the prince's side as lightly as a bubble
omnes, qui eam viderant, admirati sunt eius venustatem, motusque versantes
all who saw her wondered at her graceful, swaying movements
Propediem veste pretiosa serica et sindone indutus erat
She was very soon arrayed in costly robes of silk and muslin
et erat pulcherrima creatura in palatio
and she was the most beautiful creature in the palace
sed muta apparuit, nec loqui nec cantare poterat
but she appeared dumb, and could neither speak nor sing

erant ancillae pulchrae, sericis et auro indutae
there were beautiful female slaves, dressed in silk and gold
extiterunt et cecinerunt in conspectu domus regiae
they stepped forward and sang in front of the royal family

quilibet servus melius caneret quam proximus
each slave could sing better than the next one
Princeps autem plaudens manibus subsannavit eam
and the prince clapped his hands and smiled at her
Hoc erat maeror magnus pusillo syreni
This was a great sorrow to the little mermaid
sciebat quanto dulcius cantare poterat
she knew how much more sweetly she was able to sing
"si modo sciret, "meam vocem dimiseram cum illo".
"if only he knew I have given away my voice to be with him!"

facta est musica per orchestram
there was music being played by an orchestra
et servi exercebant choreas pulchras et pulchras
and the slaves performed some pretty, fairy-like dances
Tum parva syreni bracchia candida movit
Then the little mermaid raised her lovely white arms
quae stetit in summis digitis sicut ballerina
she stood on the tips of her toes like a ballerina
et quasi avis super aquam delabitur
and she glided over the floor like a bird over water
et saltabat cum nemo adhuc saltare potuisset
and she danced as no one yet had been able to dance
Singulis momentis magis revelatur eius pulchritudo
At each moment her beauty was more revealed
omnium blandissima, cordi erant, oculi eius expressi
most appealing of all, to the heart, were her expressive eyes
Omnes ab ea notatae sunt, praesertim Princeps
Everyone was enchanted by her, especially the prince
Princeps surdus vocaverunt eam parum exstitere
the prince called her his deaf little foundling
illaque laeta saltare, principi placere
and she happily continued to dance, to please the prince
sed recordari debemus dolorem, quem pro sua voluptate pertulit
but we must remember the pain she endured for his pleasure

omnis gradus in area sensit quasi cultros calcavit acutos
every step on the floor felt as if she trod on sharp knives

Princeps dixit se semper cum eo manere
The prince said she should remain with him always
et permissum est ad januam ejus dormiendi
and she was given permission to sleep at his door
holoserica pulvino protulerunt pro ea iacere
they brought a velvet cushion for her to lie on
et princeps habitu paginae factae pro ea
and the prince had a page's dress made for her
hoc modo posset eum comitari in equis
this way she could accompany him on horseback
Ascenderunt simul per silvas odoriferas
They rode together through the sweet-scented woods
in silvis viridibus umeros tetigere
in the woods the green branches touched their shoulders
et aviculas cantabant inter folia nova
and the little birds sang among the fresh leaves
Cum eo ad summos montium vertices ascendit
She climbed with him to the tops of high mountains
et quamvis teneros moveret pedes, risit
and although her tender feet bled, she only smiled
sequebatur eum, donec essent nubes subter eos
she followed him till the clouds were beneath them
sicut grex avium volans ad terras longinquas
like a flock of birds flying to distant lands

cum omnes dormirent, latis marmoreis sedit gradibus
when all were asleep she sat on the broad marble steps
ardentis pedes in aqua frigida lavari
it eased her burning feet to bathe them in the cold water
Tunc omnes qui in mari
It was then that she thought of all those in the sea
Quondam nocte venerunt sorores eius in brachio
Once, during the night, her sisters came up, arm in arm

cantabant moerentes nantes aqua
they sang sorrowfully as they floated on the water
Innuit ergo eis et agnoverunt eam
She beckoned to them, and they recognized her
Ipsi dixerunt ei quomodo contristaverunt sororem suam minimus
they told her how they had grieved their youngest sister
deinde omnibus noctibus ad eundem locum pervenerunt
after that, they came to the same place every night
Cum vidisset in spatio senex aviam suam
Once she saw in the distance her old grandmother
non fuerat superficies maris multos annos
she had not been to the surface of the sea for many years
rexque senexque maris pater ipse suo diademate in capite
and the old Sea King, her father, with his crown on his head
et ipse venit ubi eum videre poterat
he too came to where she could see him
manus suas tetenderunt ad eam
They stretched out their hands towards her
sed non ausi tam prope terram quam sorores
but they did not venture as near the land as her sisters

Sicut dies transierunt, amavit principem carius
As the days passed she loved the prince more dearly
et amabat eam ut amaret paruulum
and he loved her as one would love a little child
Cogitatio numquam venit ad eum ut eam faceret uxorem suam
The thought never came to him to make her his wife
sed, nisi eam duxerit, nunquam vera voluntas eius
but, unless he married her, her wish would never come true
nisi eam duceret, animam immortalem recipere non posset
unless he married her she could not receive an immortal soul
et si aliam uxorem eius somniis frangeret
and if he married another her dreams would shatter
de mane post nuptias dissolveret

on the morning after his marriage she would dissolve
et pusilla syreni fieret spuma maris
and the little mermaid would become the foam of the sea

princeps parva syreni arma
the prince took the little mermaid in his arms
et osculatus est eam in fronte sua
and he kissed her on her forehead
per oculos conata rogare illum
with her eyes she tried to ask him
"Nonne amas me omnium maxime?"
"Do you not love me the most of them all?"
"Ita, carus es mihi," princeps dixit
"Yes, you are dear to me," said the prince
"Quia habes optimum cor"
"because you have the best heart"
"et tu mihi devotissimus es".
"and you are the most devoted to me"
"Tu es sicut virgo, quam quondam vidi".
"You are like a young maiden whom I once saw"
"sed ego huic adolescentulae numquam iterum congrediar".
"but I shall never meet this young maiden again"
"in navi fracta fui";
"I was in a ship that was wrecked"
" et ejiciunt me fluctus juxta templum sanctum."
"and the waves cast me ashore near a holy temple"
"ad templum aliquot virgines virgines ministrabant".
"at the temple several young maidens performed the service"
" Minima me in litore invenerunt "
"The youngest maiden found me on the shore"
"et minimus puellarum vitam meam servavit".
"and the youngest of the maidens saved my life"
"Vidi eam, sed bis," dixit
"I saw her but twice," he explained
"et ipsa sola est in mundo quem amare possem".
"and she is the only one in the world whom I could love"

"At tu ei similis es", syreniculae parum firmavit
"But you are like her," he reassured the little mermaid
"et imaginem eius prope ex animo expulisti".
"and you have almost driven her image from my mind"
« Ad templum sanctum pertinet ».
"She belongs to the holy temple"
"Bona fortuna te pro illa ad me misit"
"good fortune has sent you instead of her to me"
"Numquam ex parte sumus", pusillum syreni consolatus est
"We will never part," he comforted the little mermaid

sed parva syreni non potuit non suspirare
but the little mermaid could not help but sigh
" nescit quod ego ipse animam suam servavi ".
"he knows not that it was I who saved his life"
"Transtuli eum ad mare ubi stat templum"
"I carried him over the sea to where the temple stands"
"Sedi sub spumis donec veniret humanus ei subvenire".
"I sat beneath the foam till the human came to help him"
"Vidi formosam virginem, quam amat";
"I saw the pretty maiden that he loves"
"Pulcherrima virgo quam me amat".
"the pretty maiden that he loves more than me"
Ingemuit valde ancilla sed flere non poterat
The mermaid sighed deeply, but she could not weep
" Ad templum sanctum pertinet virgo ";
"He says the maiden belongs to the holy temple"
"Ergo nunquam in mundum redibit".
"therefore she will never return to the world"
"Non occurrent amplius," sperata syreni parum
"they will meet no more," the little mermaid hoped
"Ego ad eum, et videbo illum cotidie".
"I am by his side and see him every day"
"Ego curabo illum et amabo illum".
"I will take care of him, and love him"
et animam meam pro eo dabo.
"and I will give up my life for his sake"

Dies Nuptialis
The Day of the Wedding

Propediem dictum est principem nupturam
Very soon it was said that the prince was going to marry
erat filia formosa vicini regis
there was the beautiful daughter of a neighbouring king
dicebatur quod uxor esset
it was said that she would be his wife
nam tum denique navis aptabatur
for the occasion a fine ship was being fitted out
Princeps dixit se solum visitare regem
the prince said he intended only to visit the king
rati tantum obviam reginae
they thought he was only going so as to meet the princess
Parva syreni risit et movit caput
The little mermaid smiled and shook her head
Cogitationes principis melius quam alii cognovit
She knew the prince's thoughts better than the others

"pereundum" dixerat ei
"I must travel," he had said to her
"Videndum est hoc pulcherrima regina"
"I must see this beautiful princess"
"Patres mei vis ire et videre illam"
"My parents want me to go and see her"
"sed non obligabunt me ut sponsam illam domum reducam".
"but they will not oblige me to bring her home as my bride"
"scis quia non possum amare eam"
"you know that I cannot love her"
"quia non est similis virgo formosa in templo".
"because she is not like the beautiful maiden in the temple"
"virginem formosam, cui tu similis es".
"the beautiful maiden whom you resemble"
"Si cogerer sponsam eligere, ego te eligerem".
"If I were forced to choose a bride, I would choose you"

"surdorum fundans, oculis illis expressis".
"my deaf foundling, with those expressive eyes"
Tunc osculatus est os suum
Then he kissed her rosy mouth
et longos agitans ludebat crines
and he played with her long, waving hair
et posuit caput in corde suo
and he laid his head on her heart
felicitatem humanam vidit et animam immortalem
she dreamed of human happiness and an immortal soul

stabant in navi nobilis navis
they stood on the deck of the noble ship
"Tu mare non times?" dixit
"You are not afraid of the sea, are you?" he said
navis ad finitimas regiones deportaret
the ship was to carry them to the neighbouring country
Tunc dixit ei procellas et tranquillitas
Then he told her of storms and of calms
dixit ei de piscibus alienis profunde sub aqua
he told her of strange fishes deep beneath the water
et narravit ei quae viderant ibi diversos
and he told her of what the divers had seen there
Illa descriptiones eius risit, leviter oblectavit
She smiled at his descriptions, slightly amused
melius sciebat quid prodigia essent in fundo maris
she knew better what wonders were at the bottom of the sea

parvum syreni sedit ornare ante lucem lunae
the little mermaid sat on the deck at moonlight
omnes conscenderant sopitos, praeterquam homo ad gubernacula
all on board were asleep, except the man at the helm
et liquidas prospexit per undas
and she gazed down through the clear water
Putavit se posse distinguere arcem patris sui

She thought she could distinguish her father's castle
et in arce posset videre aviam suam
and in the castle she could see her aged grandmother
Tunc sorores eius ex undis venerunt
Then her sisters came out of the waves
et sororem suam maeste intuebantur
and they gazed at their sister mournfully
Annuens sororibus, risit
She beckoned to her sisters, and smiled
voluit dicere quomodo felix et bene off erat
she wanted to tell them how happy and well off she was
Sed puer casulam adiit et sorores eius deiectae sunt
But the cabin boy approached and her sisters dived down
putabat quod erat spuma maris
he thought what he saw was the foam of the sea

Postero mane navis in portum ascendit
The next morning the ship got into the harbour
venissent pulcherrimam maritimum oppidum
they had arrived in a beautiful coastal town
qui venientes tintinnabula ecclesiastica salutati sunt
on their arrival they were greeted by church bells
et ex altis turribus effloruisse tubarum
and from the high towers sounded a flourish of trumpets
milites vias per quas transierunt
soldiers lined the roads through which they passed
Milites, volucribus coloribusque micantibus bayonetis
Soldiers, with flying colors and glittering bayonets
Cotidie ibi dies festus erat
Every day that they were there there was a festival
globos ac spectacula ordinata eventum
balls and entertainments were organised for the event
Sed nondum reginae speciem fecerat
But the princess had not yet made her appearance
educatus et educatus in domo religiosa
she had been brought up and educated in a religious house

discebat omnem virtutem regiae reginae
she was learning every royal virtue of a princess

Tandem regina regia speciem
At last, the princess made her royal appearance
Et pusillus syreni anxius erat videre eam
The little mermaid was anxious to see her
habuit scire an vere esset pulchra
she had to know whether she really was beautiful
et fateri oportebat eam vere pulchram esse
and she was obliged to admit she really was beautiful
eam nunquam vidi perfectiorem pulchritudinis visionem
she had never seen a more perfect vision of beauty
Pulchra erat cutis eius subtiliter
Her skin was delicately fair
et oculi caerulei ridentes veritati et puritatis nitebant
and her laughing blue eyes shone with truth and purity
"Tu," inquit princeps
"It was you," said the prince
"Tu me servavisti, cum quasi mortuus in litore iacui"
"you saved my life when I lay as if dead on the beach"
"et sponsam rubentem tenuisse in armis".
"and he held his blushing bride in his arms"

"O nimium felix sum!" inquit parvulus syreni
"Oh, I am too happy!" said he to the little mermaid
"Mea spes maxima nunc impleta"
"my fondest hopes are now fulfilled"
"Laetaberis in laetitia mea";
"You will rejoice at my happiness"
"quia tua erga me magna et sincera est";
"because your devotion to me is great and sincere"
Parva syreni manum principis osculata est
The little mermaid kissed the prince's hand
et sensit quasi iam contritum cor eius
and she felt as if her heart were already broken

mane nuptiarum eius venturum esse ad mortem
the morning of his wedding was going to bring death to her
scivit se fieri spumam maris
she knew she was to become the foam of the sea

sonus campanarum ecclesiae per villam sonabat
the sound of the church bells rang through the town
praecones per urbem equitaverunt sponsalia proclamantes
the heralds rode through the town proclaiming the betrothal
Oleum odoratum ardebat lampadibus argenteis super omni altari
Perfumed oil was burned in silver lamps on every altar
Sacerdotes in duobus turibula levaverunt
The priests waved the censers over the couple
et sponsa et sponsus iunctis manibus
and the bride and the bridegroom joined their hands
et receperunt benedictionem episcopi
and they received the blessing of the bishop
parvula syreni vestiebatur serico et auro
The little mermaid was dressed in silk and gold
sponsae vestem sustulit, magno dolore
she held up the bride's dress, in great pain
sed aures eius nihil de musica festivitate audiverunt
but her ears heard nothing of the festive music
et non viderunt oculi ejus sacram caerimoniam
and her eyes saw not the holy ceremony
Putavit de nocte mortis venientis ad eam
She thought of the night of death coming to her
et planxit omnia quae perdiderat in mundo
and she mourned for all she had lost in the world

vespere sponsa et sponsus navem conscenderunt
that evening the bride and bridegroom boarded the ship
tormenta navis rugiebant ad rem celebrandam
the ship's cannons were roaring to celebrate the event
et vexilla regni iactabant

and all the flags of the kingdom were waving
in medio navis erat tabernaculum
in the centre of the ship a tent had been erected
in tabernaculo erant lectuli dormientes pro newlyweds
in the tent were the sleeping couches for the newlyweds
venti autem ad navigandum tranquillum mare prosperi fuerunt
the winds were favourable for navigating the calm sea
et ratis lapsa caeli volucres
and the ship glided as smoothly as the birds of the sky

Cum invesperasceret, lampades coloratae accensae sunt
When it grew dark, a number of colored lamps were lighted
nautae et domus regiae in navi laetantes saltaverunt
the sailors and royal family danced merrily on the deck
Parva syreni natalem eius non adiuvare cogitas
The little mermaid could not help thinking of her birthday
quo die primum e mari surrexit
the day that she rose out of the sea for the first time
similiaque laetitiae eo die celebrabantur
similar joyful festivities were celebrated on that day
de admiratione et spe sensit illa
she thought about the wonder and hope she felt that day
cum jucundis memoriis, illa etiam in choreis iuncta
with those pleasant memories, she too joined in the dance
in pedum dolore se libravit in aere
on her paining feet, she poised herself in the air
via se insequitur hirundo cum praeda
the way a swallow poises itself when in pursued of prey
nautae et servi admirando consolati sunt
the sailors and the servants cheered her wonderingly
Numquam saltaverat tam lepide ante
She had never danced so gracefully before
Tenellae pedes sensi quasi cultris acutis secari
Her tender feet felt as if cut with sharp knives
sed pedum suorum parum curabat

but she cared little for the pain of her feet
multo acrius dolor erat cor eius penetrabilior
there was a much sharper pain piercing her heart

Sciebat hoc ultimum vesperum semper eum visurum esse
She knew this was the last evening she would ever see him
princeps cui cognatos et domum dereliquit
the prince for whom she had forsaken her kindred and home
Illa pulchram vocem ei dederat
She had given up her beautiful voice for him
et inauditum pro eo dolorem cotidie passa est
and every day she had suffered unheard-of pain for him
haec omnia passa est, doloris sui nihil noverat
she suffered all this, while he knew nothing of her pain
factum est vespere ultima esset eadem aura spirare
it was the last evening she would breath the same air as him
novissima vespera eodem sidereo spectaret caelo
it was the last evening she would gaze on the same starry sky
Ultima vespera in altum provexit
it was the last evening she would gaze into the deep sea
extremum vesperum spectabat in aetemam noctem
it was the last evening she would gaze into the eternal night
nox aeterna sine cogitationibus et somniis expectavit eam
an eternal night without thoughts or dreams awaited her
Sine anima nata est, nec unquam vincere potuit
She was born without a soul, and now she could never win one

Totum fuit gaudium et laetitia in navi usque ad mediam noctem
All was joy and gaiety on the ship until long after midnight
Risit et saltavit cum aliis in regia nave
She smiled and danced with the others on the royal ship
sed saltabat cogitatio mortis in corde suo
but she danced while the thought of death was in her heart
princeps chorus cum spectare quae habebat princeps

she had to watch the prince dance with the princess
erat spectare cum princeps osculatus est pulchram sponsam
she had to watch when the prince kissed his beautiful bride
non erat spectare eam ludere cum capilli corvi principis
she had to watch her play with the prince's raven hair
ad speculandum eos intrant tentorium, bracchium
and she had to watch them enter the tent, arm in arm

Post nuptias
After the Wedding

Et cum abiissent omnes, facti sunt adhuc in navi
After they had gone all became still on board the ship
Solus gubernator, qui ad gubernacula stabat, adhuc evigilabat
only the pilot, who stood at the helm, was still awake
parvulus syreni super ripam vasis recumbens
The little mermaid leaned on the edge of the vessel
quae respiciebat ad orientem primo rubore diluculi
she looked towards the east for the first blush of morning
radius primus aurorae, qui fuit ejus obitus
the first ray of the dawn, which was to be her death
de longe vidit sorores eius de mari
from far away she saw her sisters rising out of the sea
Tam expalluit timore quam erat
They were as pale with fear as she was
sed pulchrae comae non quassant venti
but their beautiful hair no longer waved in the wind
"Maeficae capillos nostros dedimus", dixerunt
"We have given our hair to the witch," said they
"ut hac nocte mori non habeatis"
"so that you do not have to die tonight"
"pili nostri hunc cultrum nacti sumus"
"for our hair we have obtained this knife"
"Antequam sol oritur, hoc ferro utendum est"
"Before the sun rises you must use this knife"
" cultrum in cor principis demittere debetis " ;
"you must plunge the knife into the heart of the prince"
"cadere debet calido sanguinis principis super pedes tuos".
"the warm blood of the prince must fall upon your feet"
"et tunc iterum crescent pedes tui"
"and then your feet will grow together again"
"Ubi crura habeas, caudam iterum habebis"
"where you have legs you will have a fish's tail again"

"et ubi homo eras, iterum syreni eris"
"and where you were human you will once more be a mermaid"
"tum potes vivere nobiscum sub mari".
"then you can return to live with us, under the sea"
et dabitur syreni tuis trecentis annis.
"and you will be given your three hundred years of a mermaid"
"et tunc demum in salsos spumas mutaberis".
"and only then will you be changed into the salty sea foam"
"Festina ergo: aut ipse aut ante solis exortum moriendum est".
"Haste, then; either he or you must die before sunrise"
"Avia nostra vetus noctesque diesque tibi luget".
"our old grandmother mourns for you day and night"
"caput deciduis canities"
"her white hair is falling out"
"Sicut comae nostrae ceciderunt sub forfice maleficae"
"just as our hair fell under the witch's scissors"
"Princeps occide, et veni," orabant illam
"Kill the prince, and come back," they begged her
"Nonne vides primas strictas in caelo rubras?"
"Do you not see the first red streaks in the sky?"
"Sol paucis minutis orietur, et tu morieris".
"In a few minutes the sun will rise, and you will die"
quo facto, ingemuerunt sorores eius
having done their best, her sisters sighed deeply
moesta sororum mersere sub undas
mournfully her sisters sank back beneath the waves
et sinistra parva syreni cum cultello in manibus suis
and the little mermaid was left with the knife in her hands

purpurea velum retraxit
she drew back the crimson curtain of the tent
et in tabernaculo vidit sponsam pulchram
and in the tent she saw the beautiful bride

faciem stabat super pectus principis
her face was resting on the prince's breast
et tunc parvulus syreni aspexit caelum
and then the little mermaid looked at the sky
in prospectu roseo aurora clarior et clarior increbuit
on the horizon the rosy dawn grew brighter and brighter
At illa in manibus acutum cultrum attigerat
She glanced at the sharp knife in her hands
et rursus ad principis oculos defixit
and again she fixed her eyes on the prince
Inclinavit et osculatus est frontem nobilem
She bent down and kissed his noble brow
susurravit nomen sponsae in somnis
he whispered the name of his bride in his dreams
somniabat princeps duxerat
he was dreaming of the princess he had married
cultellus tremuit in manu pusilli syreni
the knife trembled in the hand of the little mermaid
sed cultrum in mare se proiecit
but she flung the knife far into the sea

ubi ferrum cecidit aqua rubra
where the knife fell the water turned red
guttae quae eiti sunt quasi sanguinem
the drops that spurted up looked like blood
Unum extremum ejecit vultus in principem quem amabat
She cast one last look upon the prince she loved
sol caelum aureis sagittis
the sun pierced the sky with its golden arrows
et proiecit se de navi in mare
and she threw herself from the ship into the sea
pusillus syreni sensit corpus dissolutum in spumam
the little mermaid felt her body dissolving into foam
et omnia que ascenderunt super faciem erant bullae aeris
and all that rose to the surface were bubbles of air
radiis calidis solis frigora

the sun's warm rays fell upon the cold foam
sed non sentiebat quasi moreretur
but she did not feel as if she were dying
mirum in modum percepit calorem solis lucidi
in a strange way she felt the warmth of the bright sun
quae vidit centum creaturae pulchrae diaphanum
she saw hundreds of beautiful transparent creatures
creaturae volabant in circuitu eius
the creatures were floating all around her
per creaturas videre vela navium
through the creatures she could see the white sails of the ships
interque vela navium purpureis vidit in aethere nimbis
and between the sails of the ships she saw the red clouds in the sky
Eorum oratio canorus et puerilis fuit
Their speech was melodious and childlike
sed non exaudiri mortalium aures eorum oratio
but their speech could not be heard by mortal ears
nec corporibus oculis mortalia videri
nor could their bodies be seen by mortal eyes
Parva syreni percepit eam similem esse
The little mermaid perceived that she was like them
et sensit altius et altius surgere
and she felt that she was rising higher and higher
"Ubi sum?" quaesivit, et sonuit vox aetherea
"Where am I?" asked she, and her voice sounded ethereal
nulla est musica terrena quae eam possit imitari
there is no earthly music that could imitate her
respondit una ex illis, "Vos estis in filiabus caeli."
"you are among the daughters of the air," answered one of them
"Ancilla immortalem animam non habet"
"A mermaid has not an immortal soul"
" neque opes immortales consequi posse Nereides ".
"nor can mermaids obtain immortal souls"
"nisi vincit amor hominis"

"unless she wins the love of a human being"
" in alterius voluntate fatum suum aeternae sortis " ;
"on the will of another hangs her eternal destiny"
"similis es, aut immortales animas non habemus".
"like you, we do not have immortal souls either"
"sed factis nostris immortalem animam consequi possumus".
"but we can obtain an immortal soul by our deeds"
"Nos in calidas terras volamus et aestuosae caeli refrigeramur".
"We fly to warm countries and cool the sultry air"
"Calor qui hominem pestilentia destruit"
"the heat that destroys mankind with pestilence"
" Unguentum florum portamus " ;
"We carry the perfume of the flowers"
"et salutem et restitutionem diffundimus".
"and we spread health and restoration"

"Trecentos annos mundum sic iteramus"
"for three hundred years we travel the world like this"
"in tempore illo omne bonum facere in nostra potestate nitimur".
"in that time we strive to do all the good in our power"
"si obtinemus immortalem animam accipimus"
"if we succeed we receive an immortal soul"
"et tunc etiam nos felicitati hominum participamus".
"and then we too take part in the happiness of mankind"
"Tu, miselle Syre, optime fecisti".
"You, poor little mermaid, have done your best"
"Conatus es ex toto corde facere sicut nos facere"
"you have tried with your whole heart to do as we are doing"
"Magnum passus es et pertuli dolorem".
"You have suffered and endured an enormous pain"
"per bona opera tua te ipsum spiritui mundo extulisti".
"by your good deeds you raised yourself to the spirit world"
" et nunc per trecentos annos habitabis " .
"and now you will live alongside us for three hundred years"

"conciliando sicut nos immortalem animam consequaris".
"by striving like us, you may obtain an immortal soul"
Parva syreni oculos suos glorificatos ad solem levavit
The little mermaid lifted her glorified eyes toward the sun
primum percepit, lacrimis oculosque repletos
for the first time, she felt her eyes filling with tears

In navi egressa erat vita et strepitus
On the ship she had left there was life and noise
vidit principem et sponsam pulcherrimam quaerendo illam
she saw the prince and his beautiful bride searching for her
Triste intuentes spumis margaritis
Sorrowfully, they gazed at the pearly foam
quasi scirent se in undas projecisse
it was as if they knew she had thrown herself into the waves
Invisibilia, frontem sponsae osculata est
Unseen, she kissed the forehead of the bride
et resurrexit cum aliis filiis aeris
and then she rose with the other children of the air
simul ascenderunt roseo nubem quae supernatavit
together they went to a rosy cloud that floated above

"Post trecentos annos" unus ex illis explicare coepit
"After three hundred years," one of them started explaining
" tunc natabimus in regnum caelorum "
"then we shall float into the kingdom of heaven," said she
"Et licet illuc citius perveniamus", insusurravit comes
"And we may even get there sooner," whispered a companion
"Invisos domos ingredi possumus ubi infantes sunt";
"Unseen we can enter the houses where there are children"
"in quibusdam domibus invenimus bonos filios".
"in some of the houses we find good children"
"Hi filii sunt gaudium parentum".
"these children are the joy of their parents"
"et hi filii amore parentum merentur".
"and these children deserve the love of their parents"

"Tales pueri tempus nostrae probationis minuunt".
"such children shorten the time of our probation"
"puer non scit cum per cubiculum volamus"
"The child does not know when we fly through the room"
"et non sciunt quod rideamus cum gaudio in bonis eorum".
"and they don't know that we smile with joy at their good conduct"
"quia tunc judicium nostrum citius venit una die".
"because then our judgement comes one day sooner"
"At etiam liberos nequam ac nefarios videmus".
"But we see naughty and wicked children too"
"Cum tales videmus lacrimas moeroris effundimus".
"when we see such children we shed tears of sorrow"
et omni lachryma dies additur tempori .
"and for every tear we shed a day is added to our time"

www.ingramcontent.com/pod-product-compliance
Lightning Source LLC
Chambersburg PA
CBHW012008090526
44590CB00026B/3930